Hello	2	6 On the farm	58
1 My classroom	8	7 I'm hungry!	68
2 My family	18	8 All aboard!	78
3 My face	28	9 Party clothes	88
4 Toys	38	Cutouts	99
5 My house	48		

Hello

1 Match and say the names.

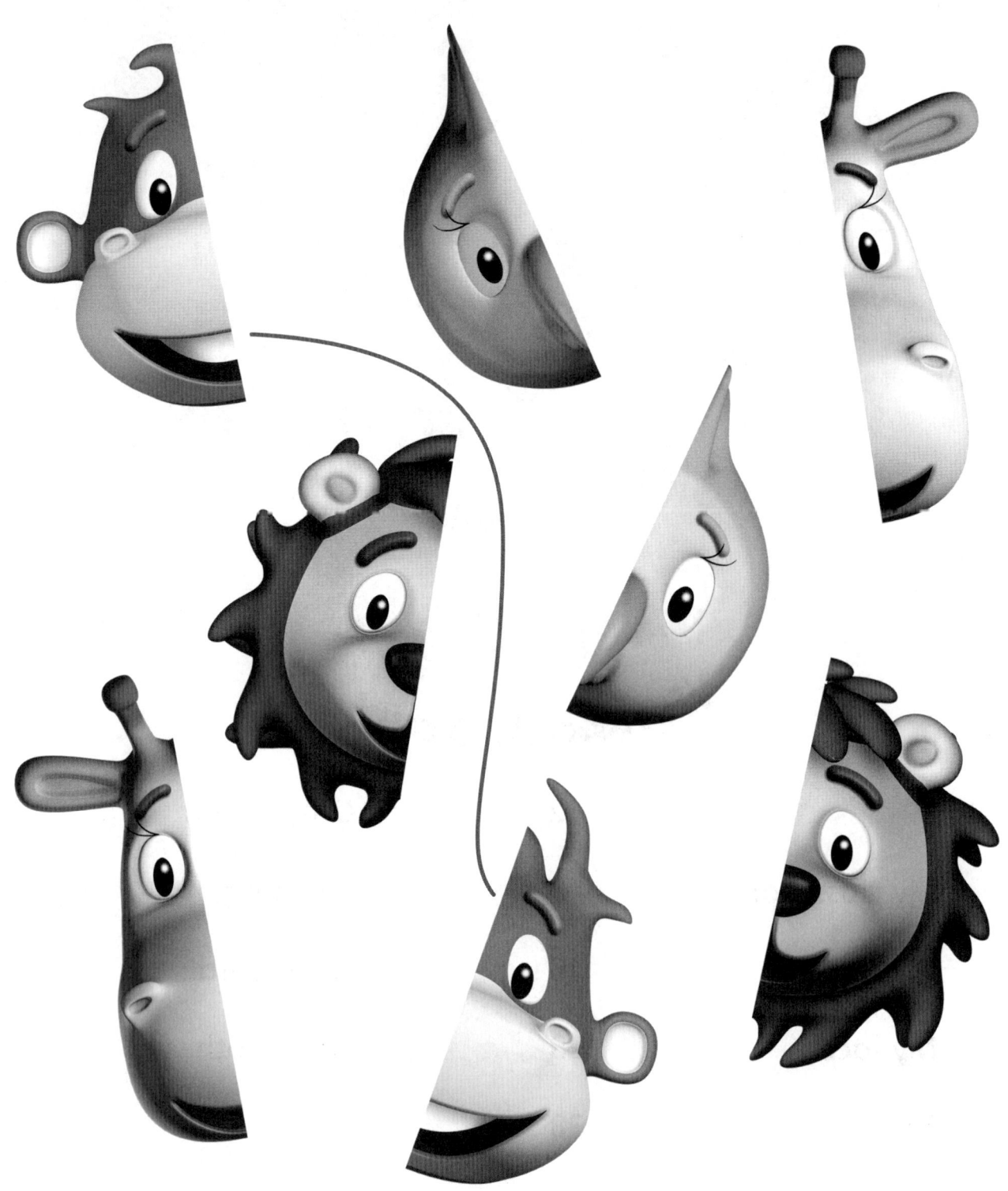

1 Trace and match.

Practice 3

1  **Listen and trace.**

①

②

③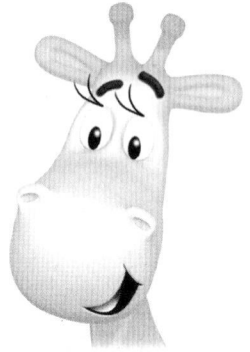

④

4 I'm (Mike, Leo, Gina, Polly).

1 Listen and color.

red, blue, green, orange, purple, yellow

5

1 Think! **Look and color.**

1

2

6 Value: saying *sorry*

1 Color. Say the words.

2 Draw faces. ☺ 😐 ☹

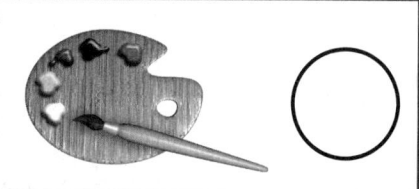

Review 7

1 My classroom

1 Find and color.

pencil, chair, bag, eraser, book, desk

1 CD1 14 Listen and circle.

1

2

3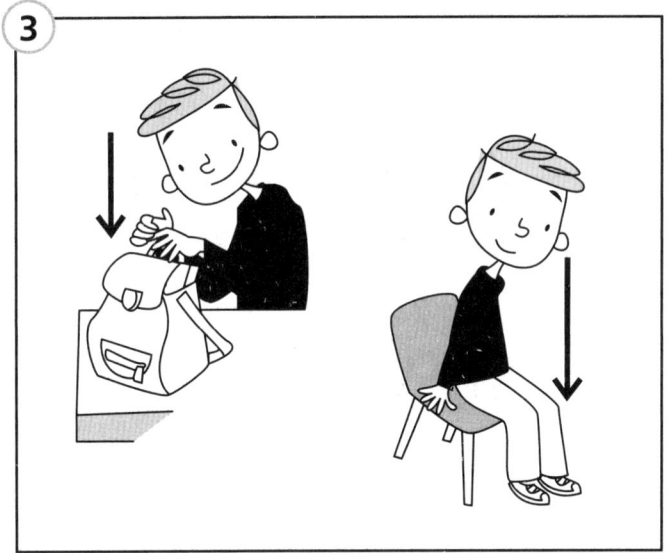

4

5

6

Stand up. Sit down. Open ... Close ... Pick up ... Put ...

1 Draw and color.

10 Practice

1 **Think!** Count and match.

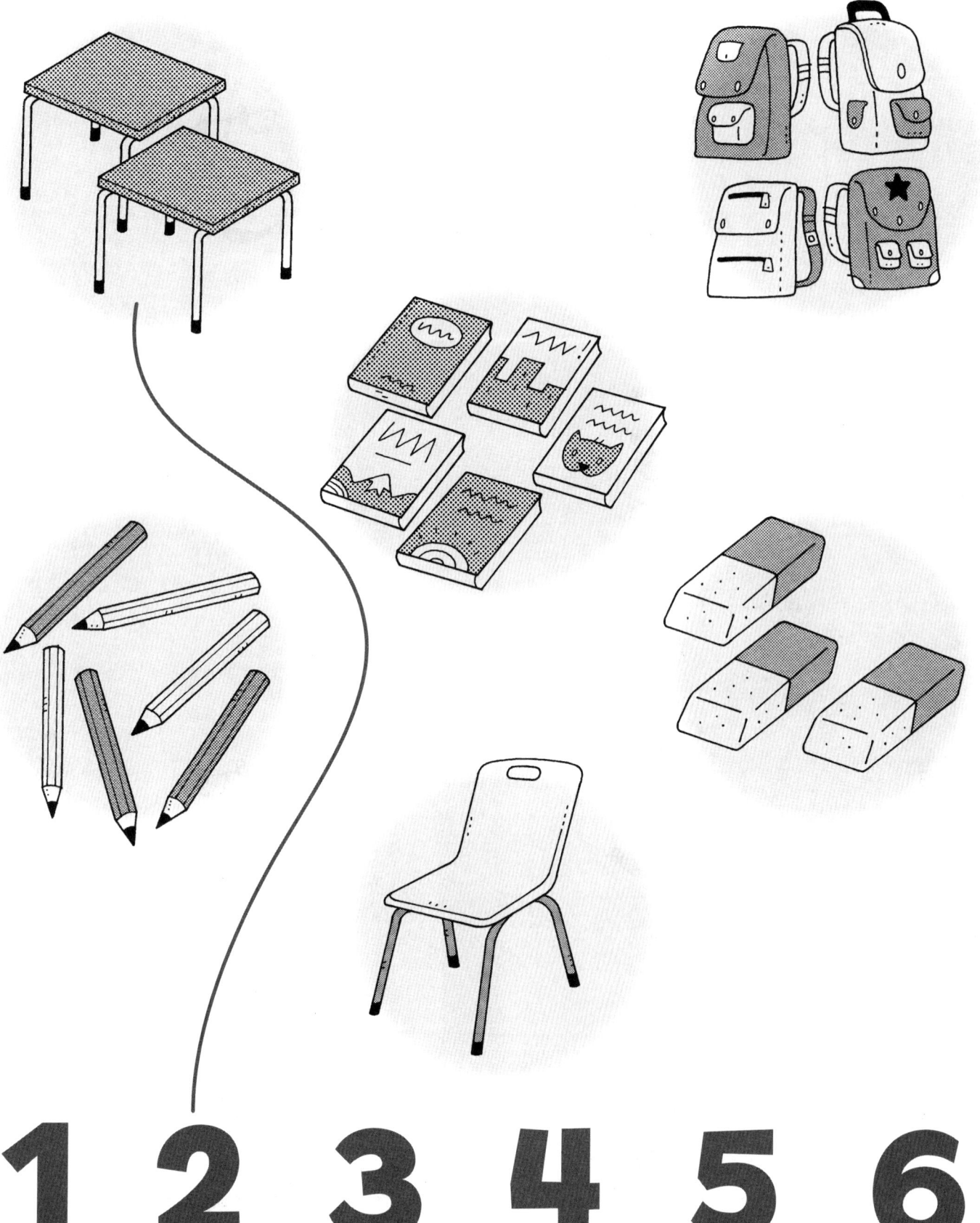

1 2 3 4 5 6

one, two, three, four, five, six

1 🎧 CD1 19 Listen and trace.

1.

2.

3.

4.

1 Think! **Look and color.**

1

2

Value: lending 13

1  **Listen and color. Color to match.**

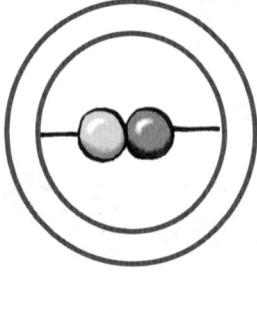

School

 **Look and circle.**

School 15

1 Make a collage.

1 Say the words. Color the circles.

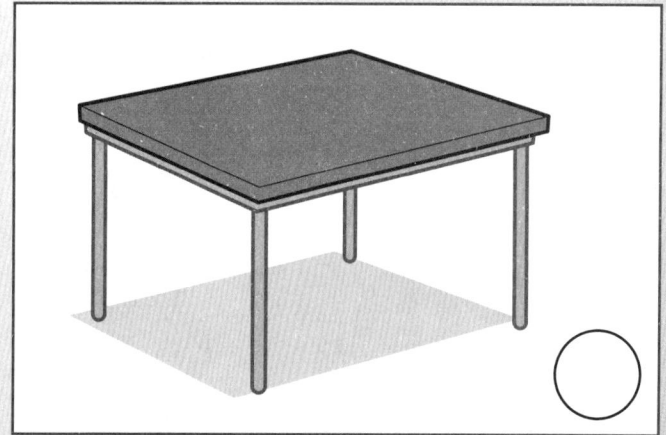
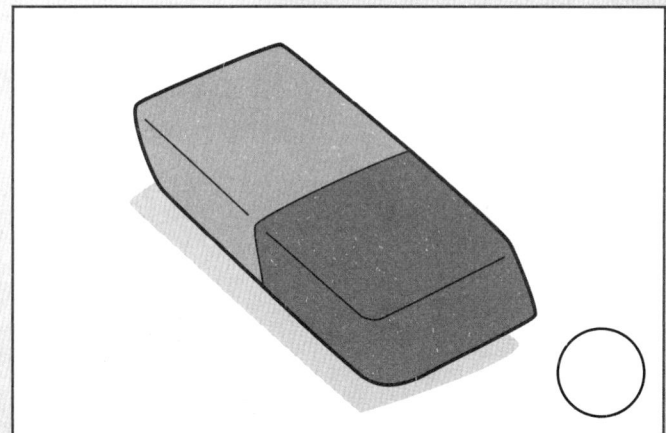

2 Draw faces. 😊 😐 ☹

2 My family

1 Circle and say the words.

grandpa, grandma, mom, dad, sister, brother

1 🎧 CD1 26 Listen and circle.

1

3

4

5

6

This is my (brother), (Tom).

1 Point and say the names and the words.

1

2

3

4

5

6

1 Draw lines. Color and make sentences.

This is my (book). 21

1 Listen and trace.

1.

2.

3.

4.

1 Think! **Look and color.**

1

2

Value: sharing 23

1 Look and draw.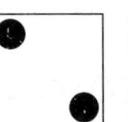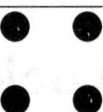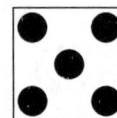

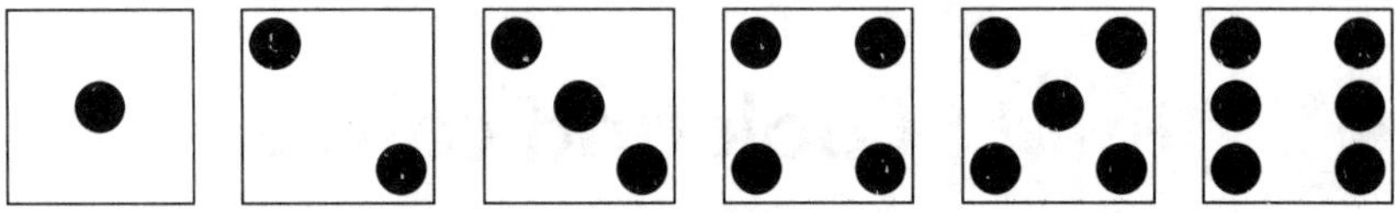

24 Social studies

1 Think! **Look and say the family words.**

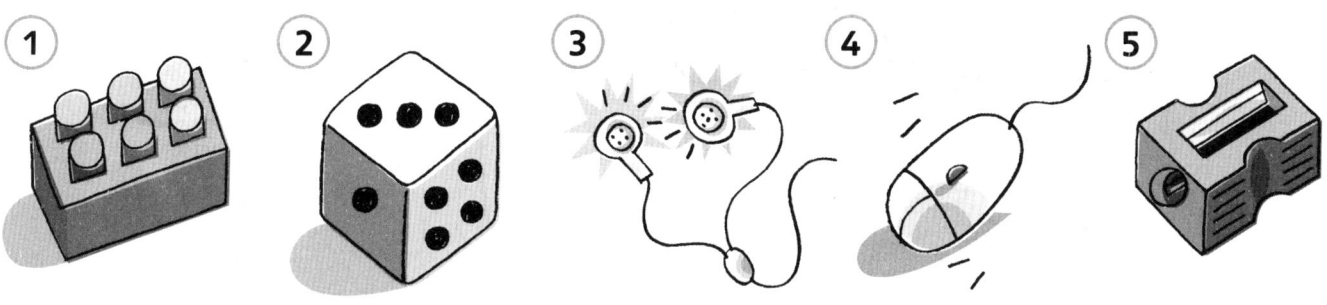

Social studies 25

1 Make an ice pop stick family.

26 Creativity

1 Say the words. Color the circles.

2 Draw faces. 🙂 😐 ☹

Review 27

3 My face

1 Color the clown.

2 Describe your clown. Color your friend's clown.

28 eyes, ears, nose, face, teeth, mouth

1 **Think!** Look, draw, and say the words.

I'm/You're (angry, happy, sad, scared).

1 How are you feeling today? Complete the face.

30 Practice

1 **Listen and circle.**

1

2

3

4

Are you (angry)? Yes, I am. / No, I'm not.

1  Listen and trace.

1

2

3

4

Story practice

1 Think! **Look and color.**

1

2

Value: don't play tricks   33

1 Think! Connect the dots and answer.

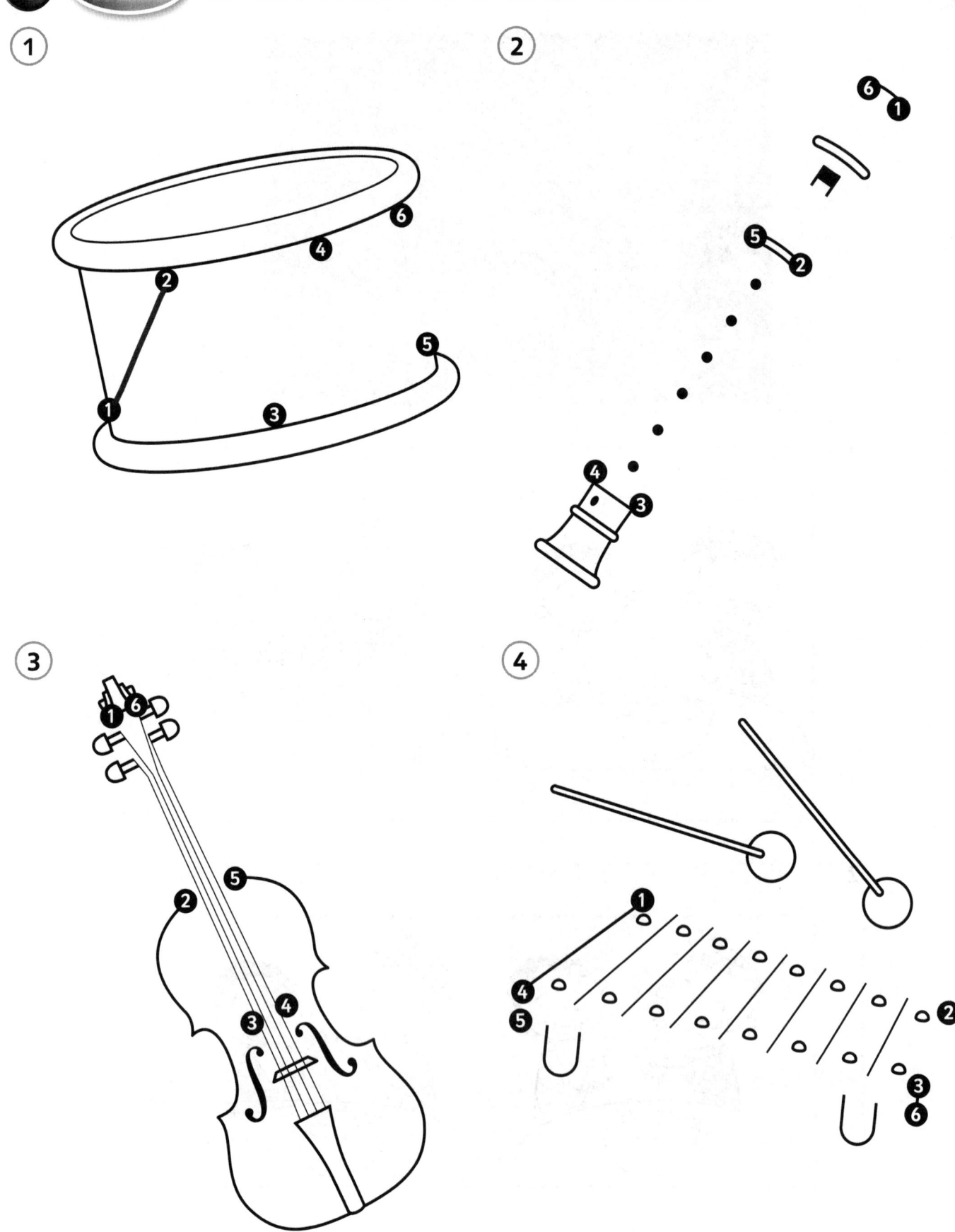

1 **Think!** Look and draw.

Music 35

1 Make a xylophone.

1 Say the words. Color the circles.

2 Draw faces. 😊 😐 ☹

Review 37

4 Toys

1 **Think!** Count and match.

1 2 3 4 5 6

38 ball, kite, jump rope, teddy bear, doll, plane

1 Draw four toys.

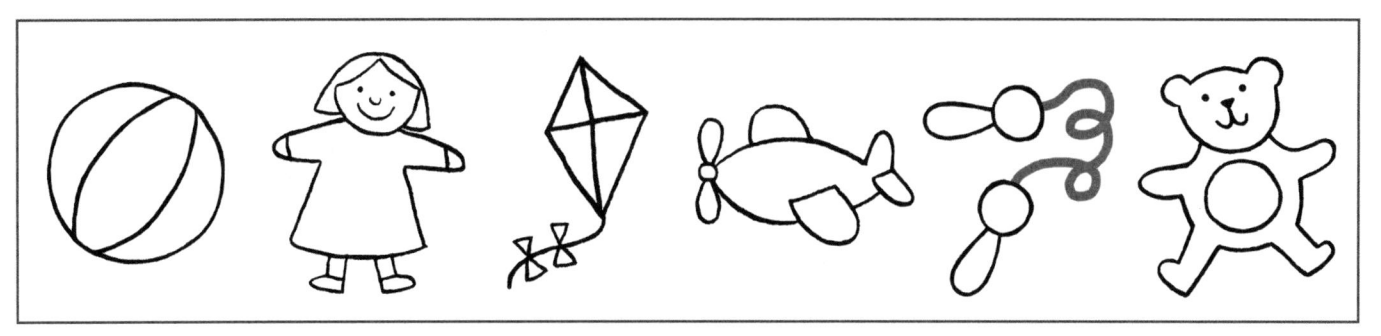

2 Describe your picture. Draw your friend's picture.

I have a (ball).

1 Complete the toys. Draw the missing toy.

1 🎧 CD1 53 **Listen and color.**

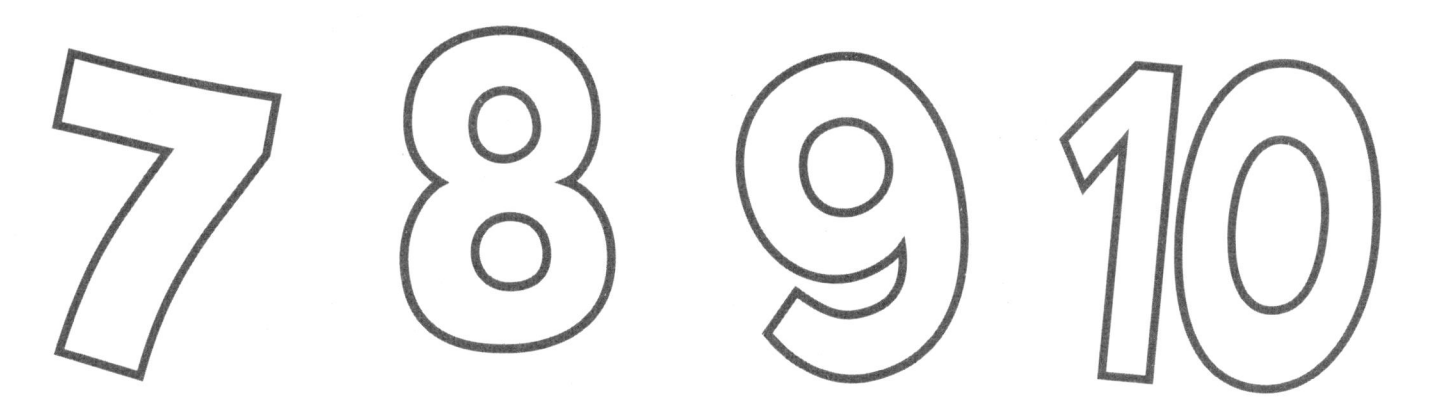

7 8 9 10

2 *Think!* **Count and draw.**

7	8
9	10

seven, eight, nine, ten 41

1 🎧 CD1 55 **Listen and trace.**

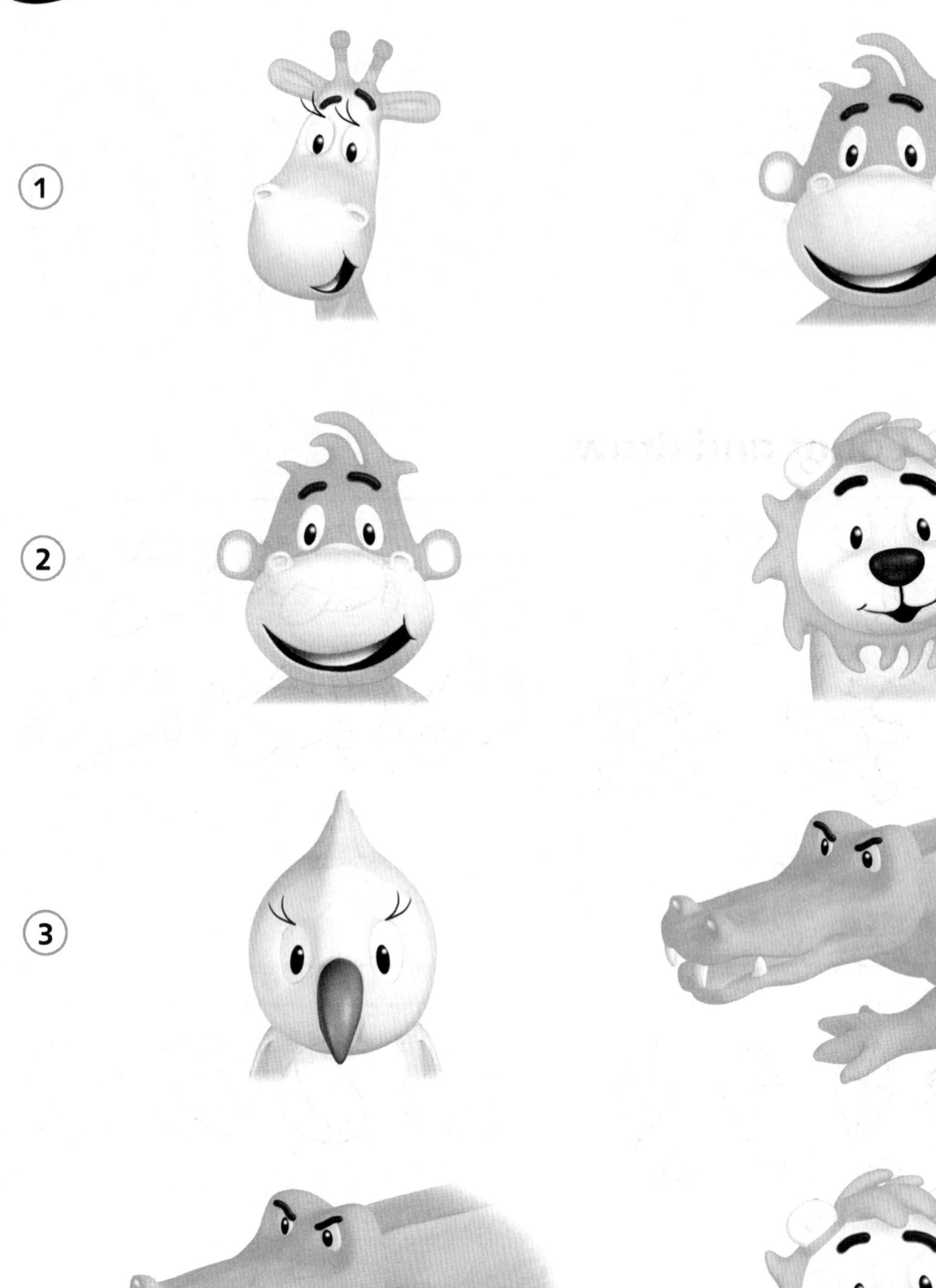

①

②

③

④

42 Story practice

1 **Think!** Look and color.

Value: working together

1 Look and draw two jump ropes and three balls.

1 Think! Look and circle red and blue.

Physical education 45

1 Make a paper plane.

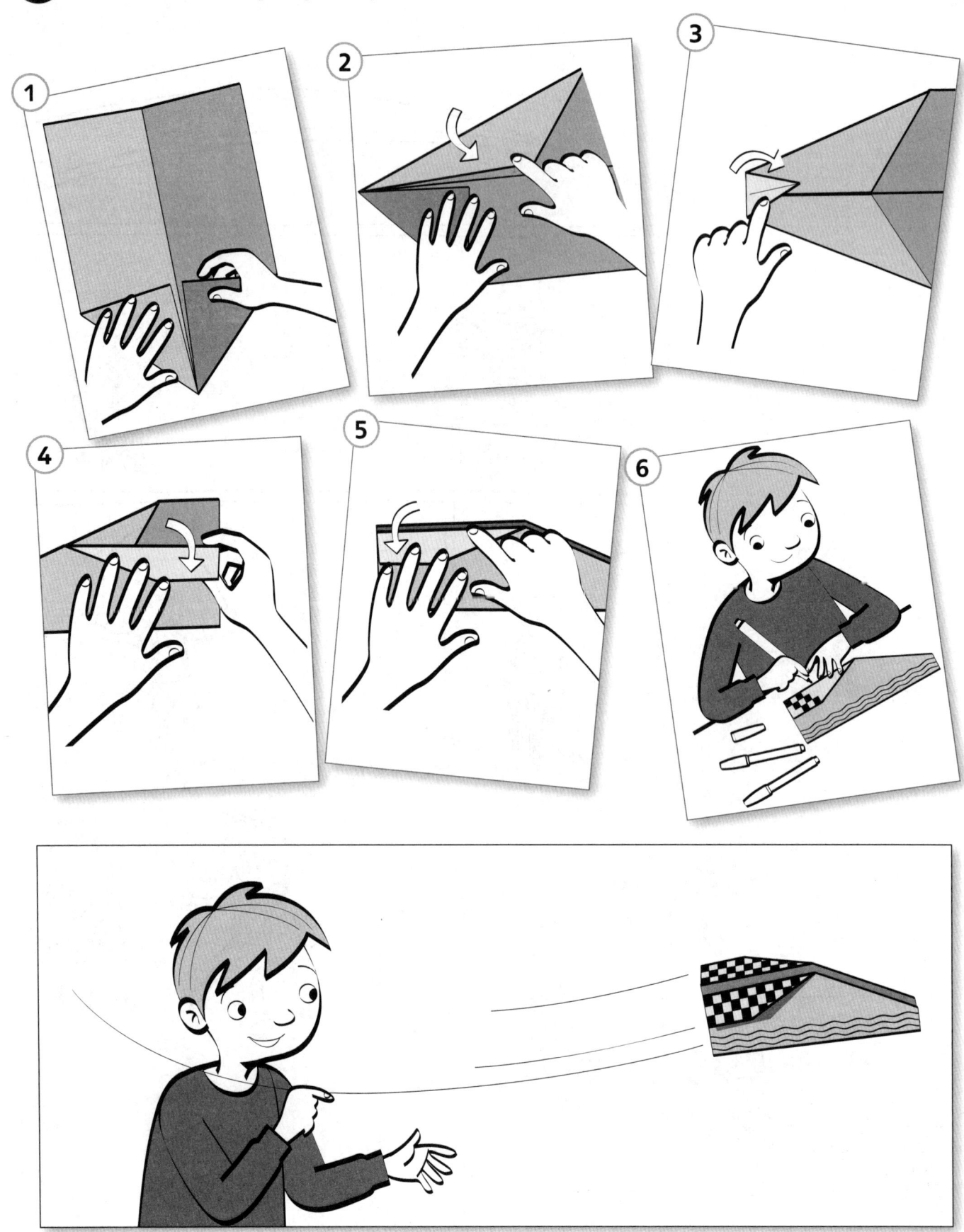

46 Creativity

1 Say the words. Color the circles.

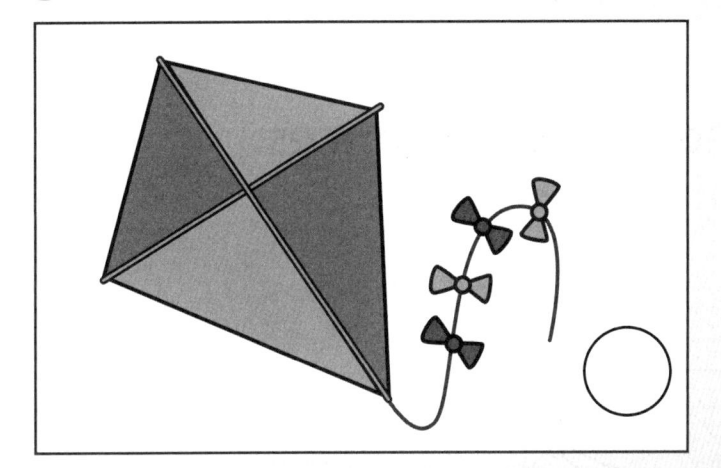

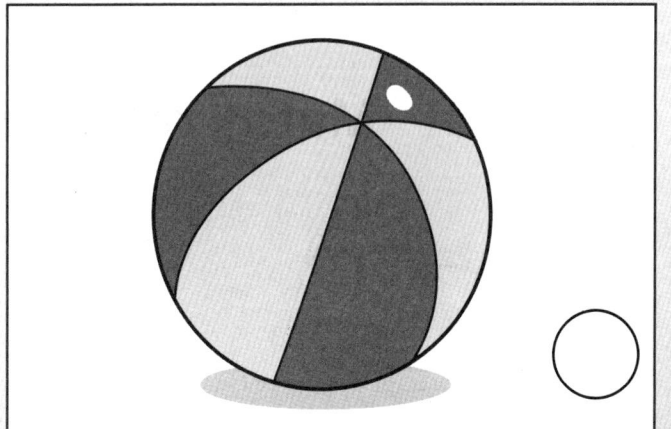

2 Draw faces. 😊 😐 ☹

Review 47

5 My house

1 Think! Match, color, and make sentences.

bathtub

couch

cabinet

armchair

bed

table

bathtub, cabinet, bed, couch, table, armchair

1 **Listen and circle.**

in, on, under

1 **Draw lines.**

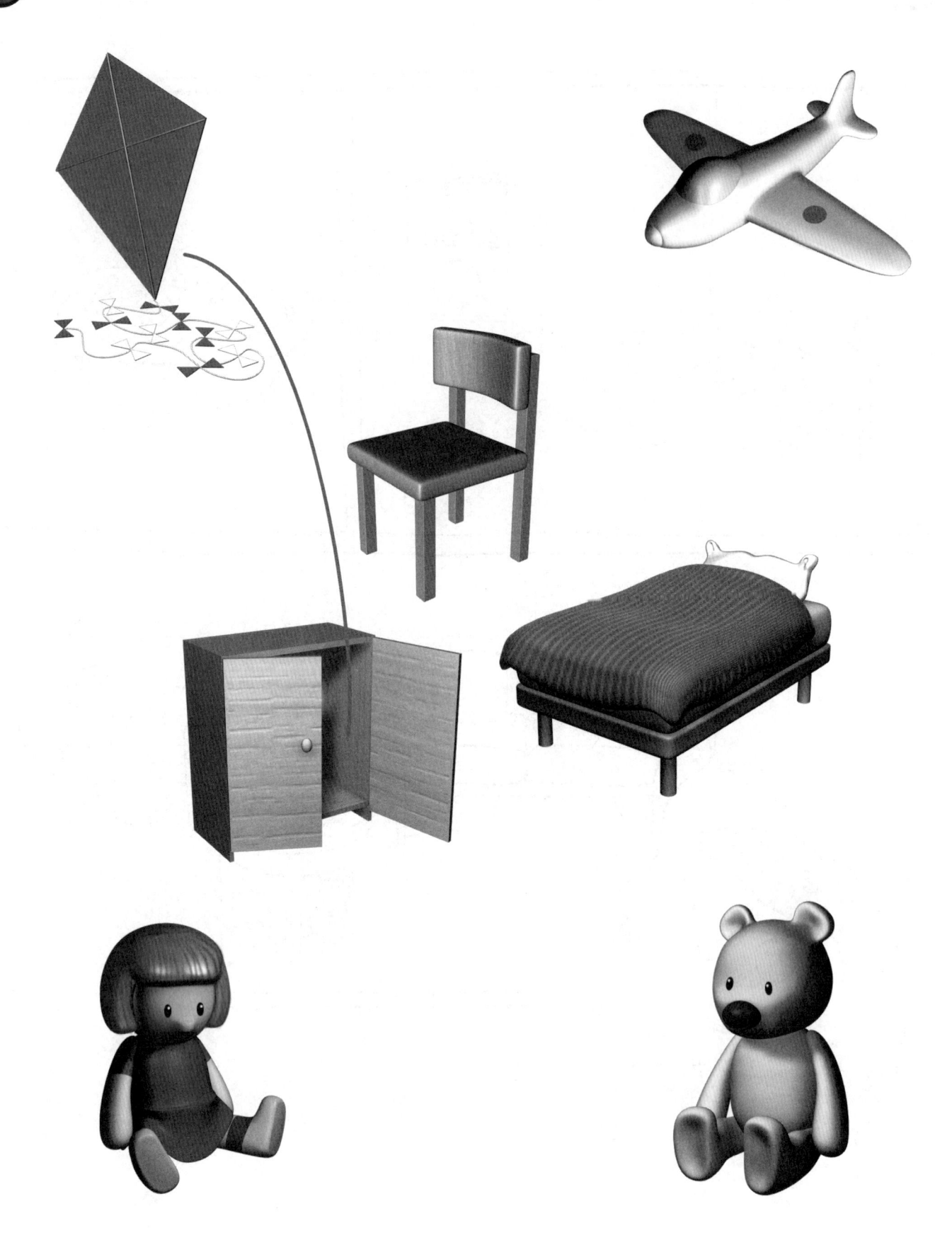

1 Find pairs and circle.

The (doll) is (in) the (bathtub).

51

1 Listen and trace.

1
2
3
4

52 Story practice

1 **Think!** Look and color.

1

2

Value: listening to people 53

1 🎧 **Listen and color.**

| 1 | 2 | 3 | 4 | 5 | 6 |

2 (Think!) **Look and color.**

54 Geography

1 **Think!** Follow the path. Count and circle.

1 2 3 4 5 6 7 8 9 10

Geography

1 Make dollhouse furniture.

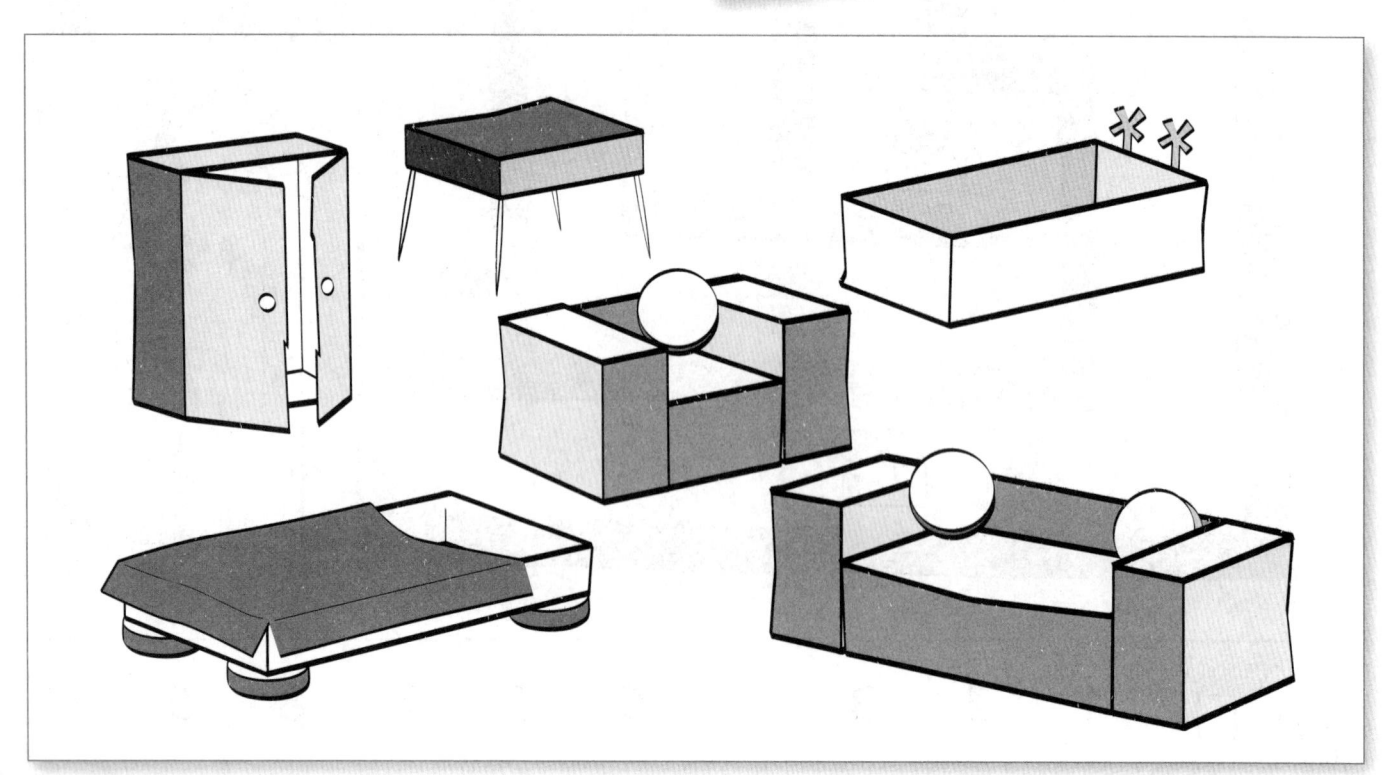

Creativity

1 Say the words and trace. Color the circles.

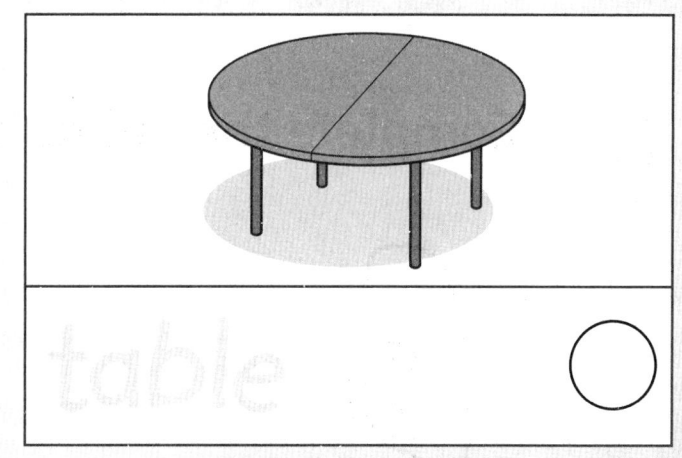

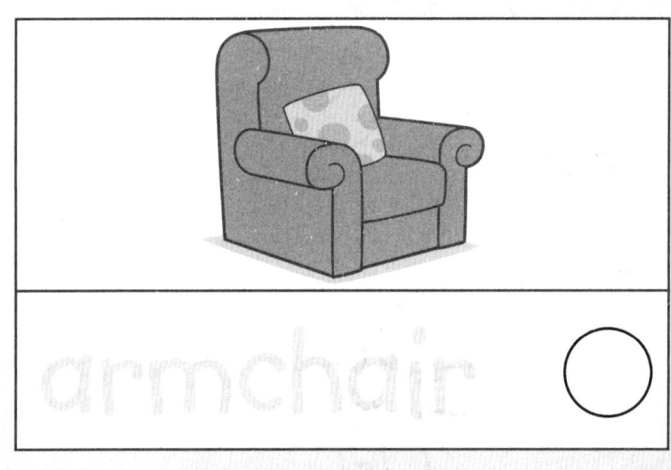

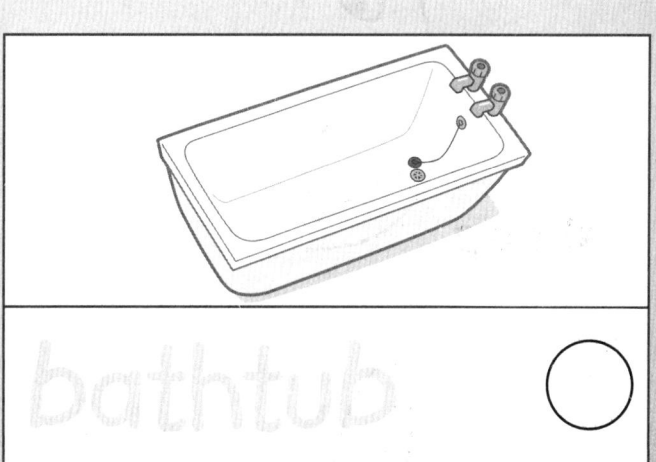

bed ○

table ○

armchair ○

cabinet ○

couch ○

bathtub ○

2 Draw faces. ☺ 😐 ☹

Review 57

6 On the farm

1 Complete the animals. Say the words.

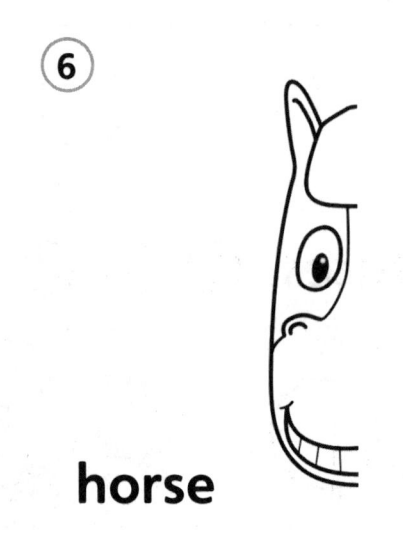

1. dog
2. cat
3. sheep
4. cow
5. rabbit
6. horse

58 cat, horse, cow, dog, rabbit, sheep

1 Draw your favorite animals.

(two) sheep, three (cat)s, I like (cats)

1 **Listen, point, and say the words.**

1 🎧 CD2 20 **Listen and color. Follow the paths.**

My favorite color is (blue) / (toys) are (planes).

1 Listen and trace.

1.

2.

3.

4.

62 Story practice

1 **Think!** Look and color.

Value: paying compliments   63

1 Match. Where do they live?

1 Think! **Look and cross out.**

1 Make a woolly sheep.

66 Creativity

1 Say the words and trace. Color the circles.

dog cat

sheep cow

rabbit horse

2 Draw faces. 😊 😐 ☹

Review 67

7 I'm hungry!

1 Think! Look, draw, and say the words.

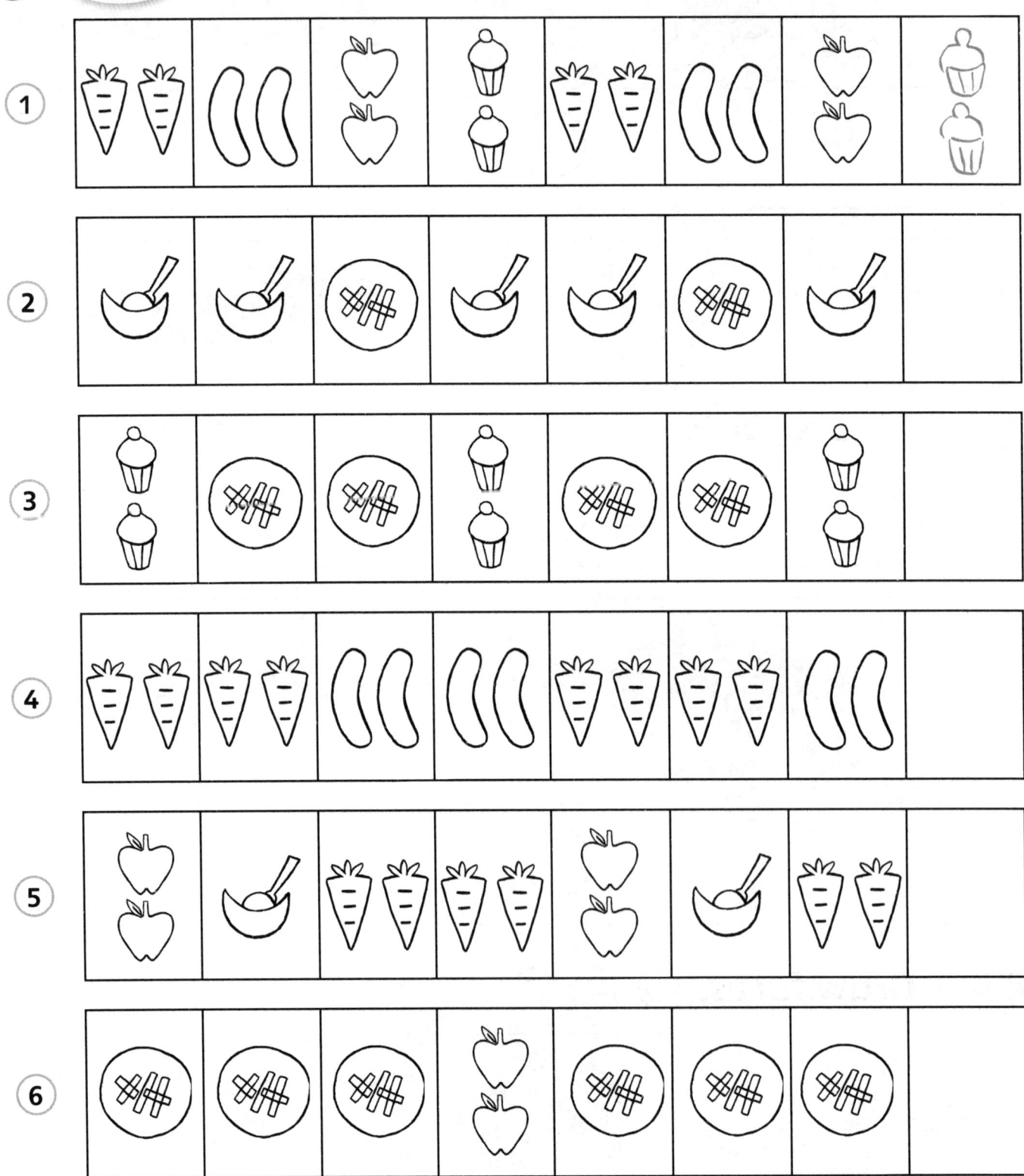

68 carrots, sausages, apples, cupcakes, ice cream, fries

7

1 🎧 CD2 28 **Listen and match.**

1.
2.
3.
4.

2 **Draw your favorite food.**

I like / I don't like (carrots).   69

1 **Draw.**

1 Draw faces. 🙂 🙁   Tell your friend and draw.

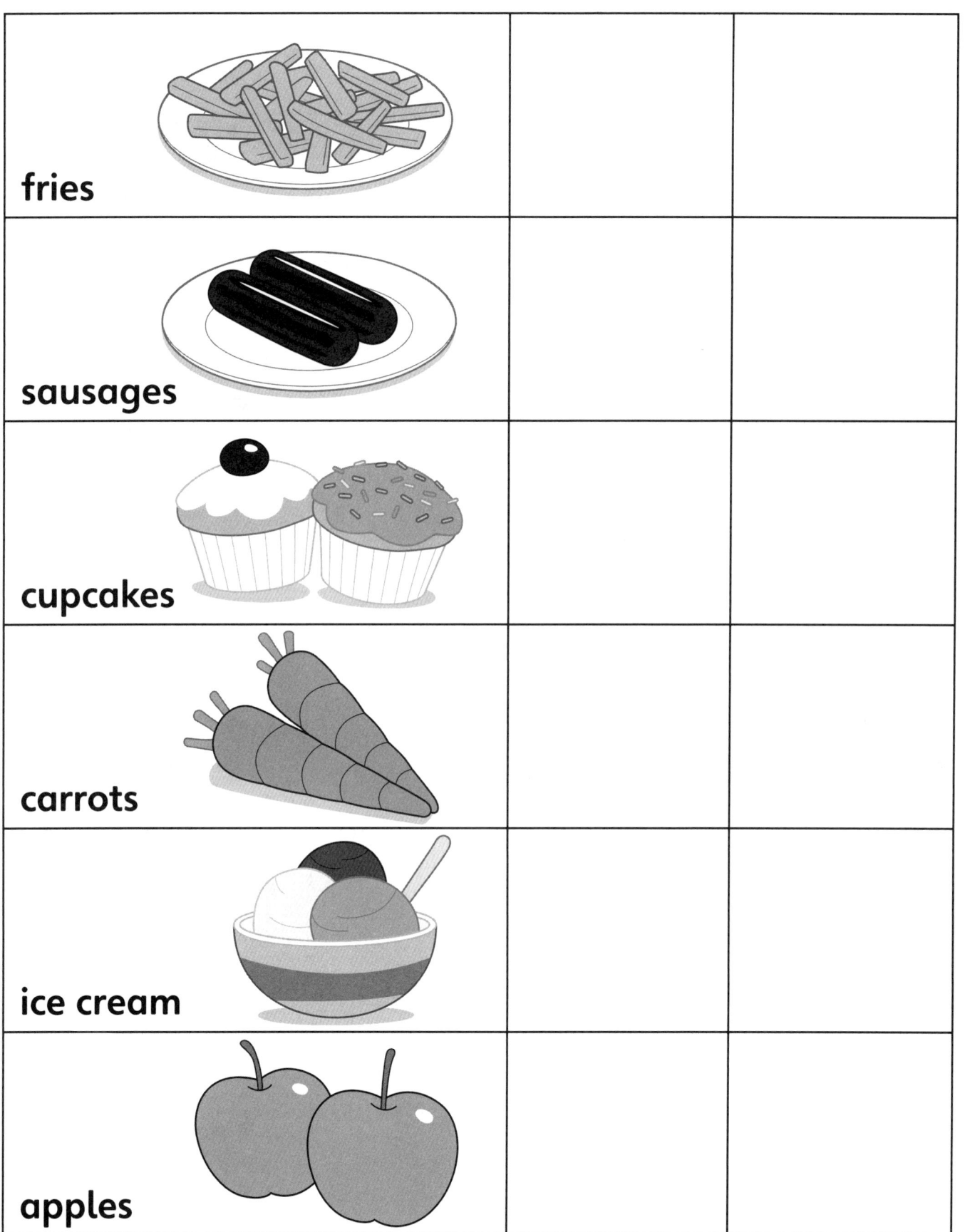

fries			
sausages			
cupcakes			
carrots			
ice cream			
apples			

I like / I don't like (blue/cats/dolls).

1 🎧 CD2 32 **Listen and trace.**

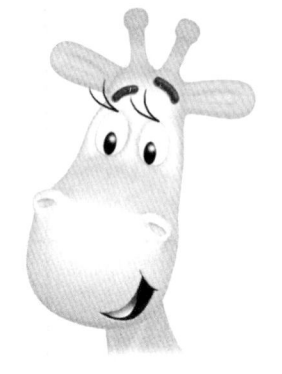

72 Story practice

1 Think! **Look and color.**

1

2

Value: don't be greedy   73

1 Draw lines. Describe the meals.

74 Science

1 **Think!** **Look and circle.**

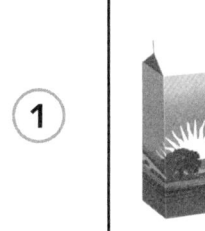

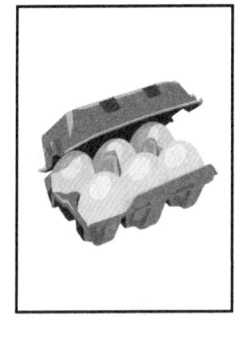

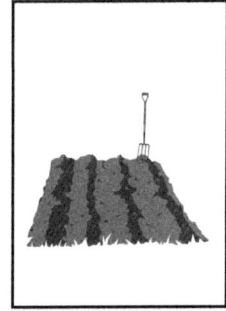

1 Make cookie faces.

76 Creativity

1 Say the words and trace. Color the circles.

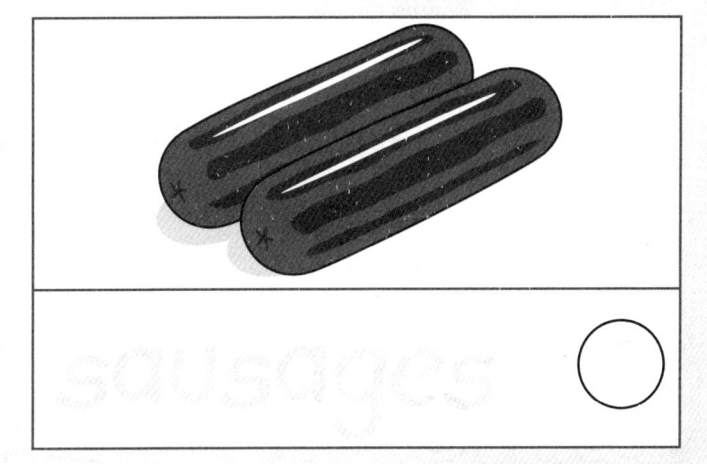

carrots

sausages

apples

cupcakes

ice cream

fries

2 Draw faces. 😊 😐 ☹

Review 77

8 All aboard!

1 Think! Match, color, and make sentences.

car

bike

scooter

bus

boat

train

78 boat, train, car, scooter, bus, bike

1 Follow the lines. Make sentences.

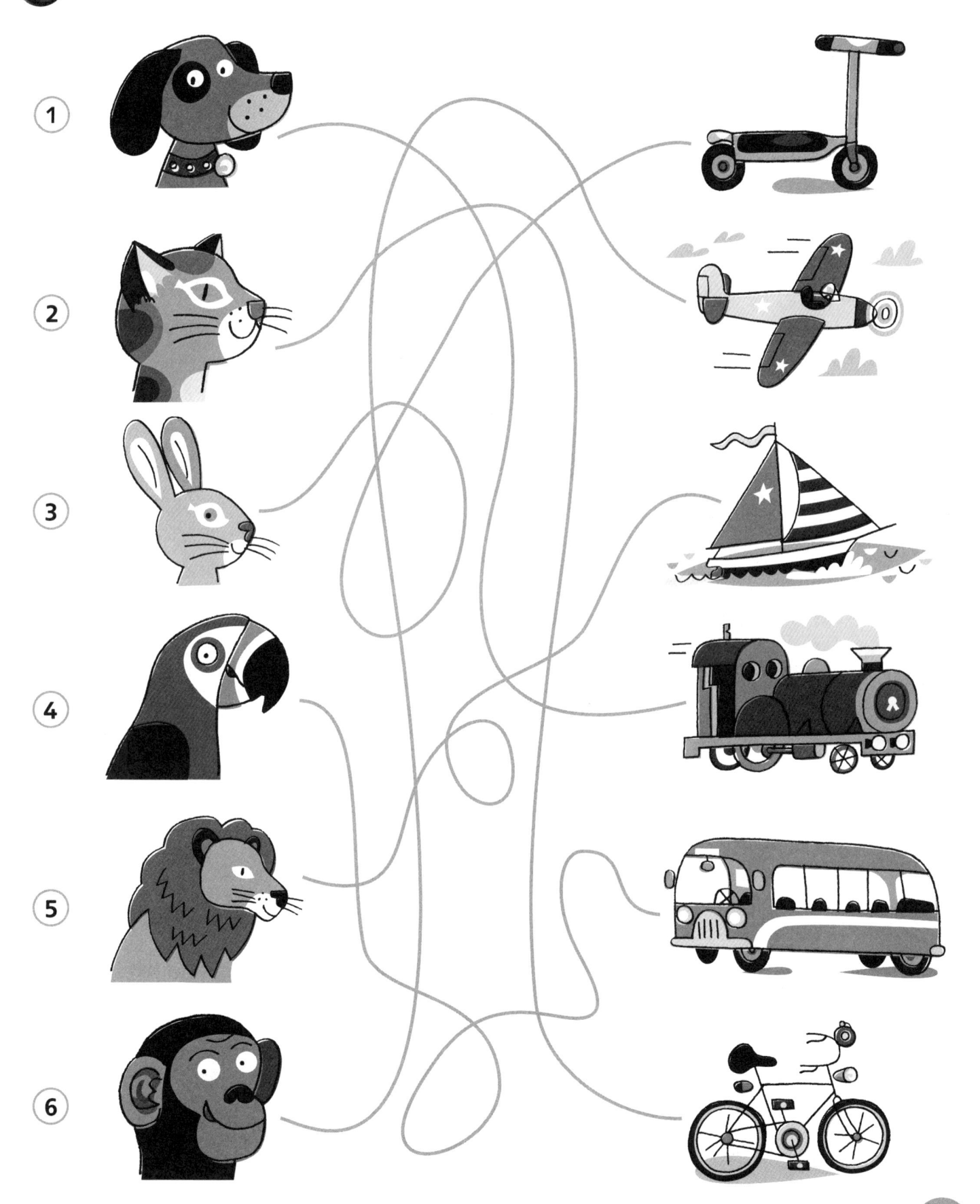

I'm driving/flying/riding/sailing.

1 🎧 CD2 40 **Listen, point, and say the words.**

1 🎧 CD2 42 Think! Listen and circle.

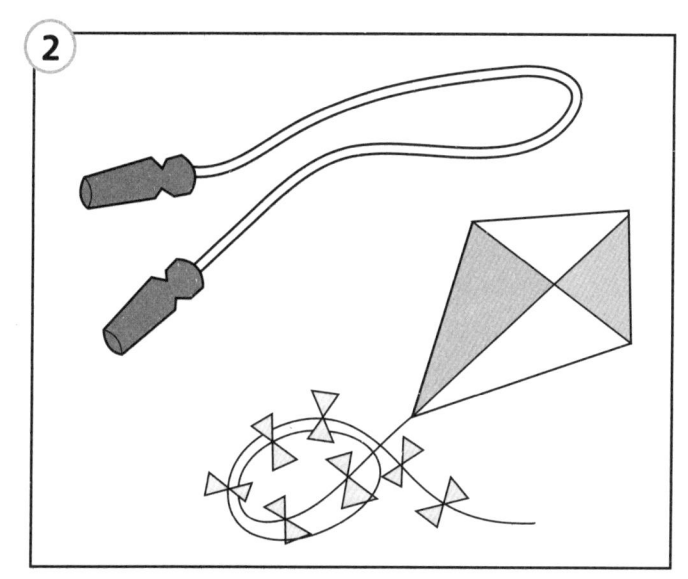

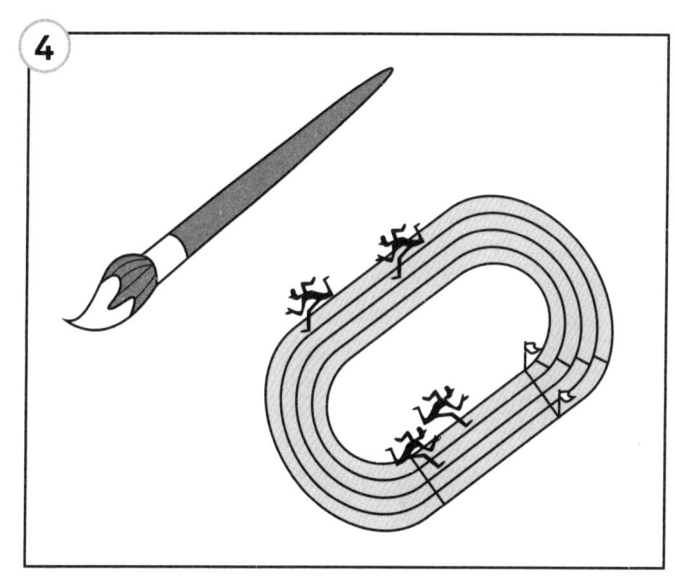

flying a kite, swimming, climbing a tree, running, brushing my teeth, washing my hands

1 🄲🄳🄲 **Listen and trace.**

1.

2.

3.

4.

82 Story practice

1 **Think!** Look and color.

1

2

Value: saying *thank you* — 83

1 Trace with four colors to match.

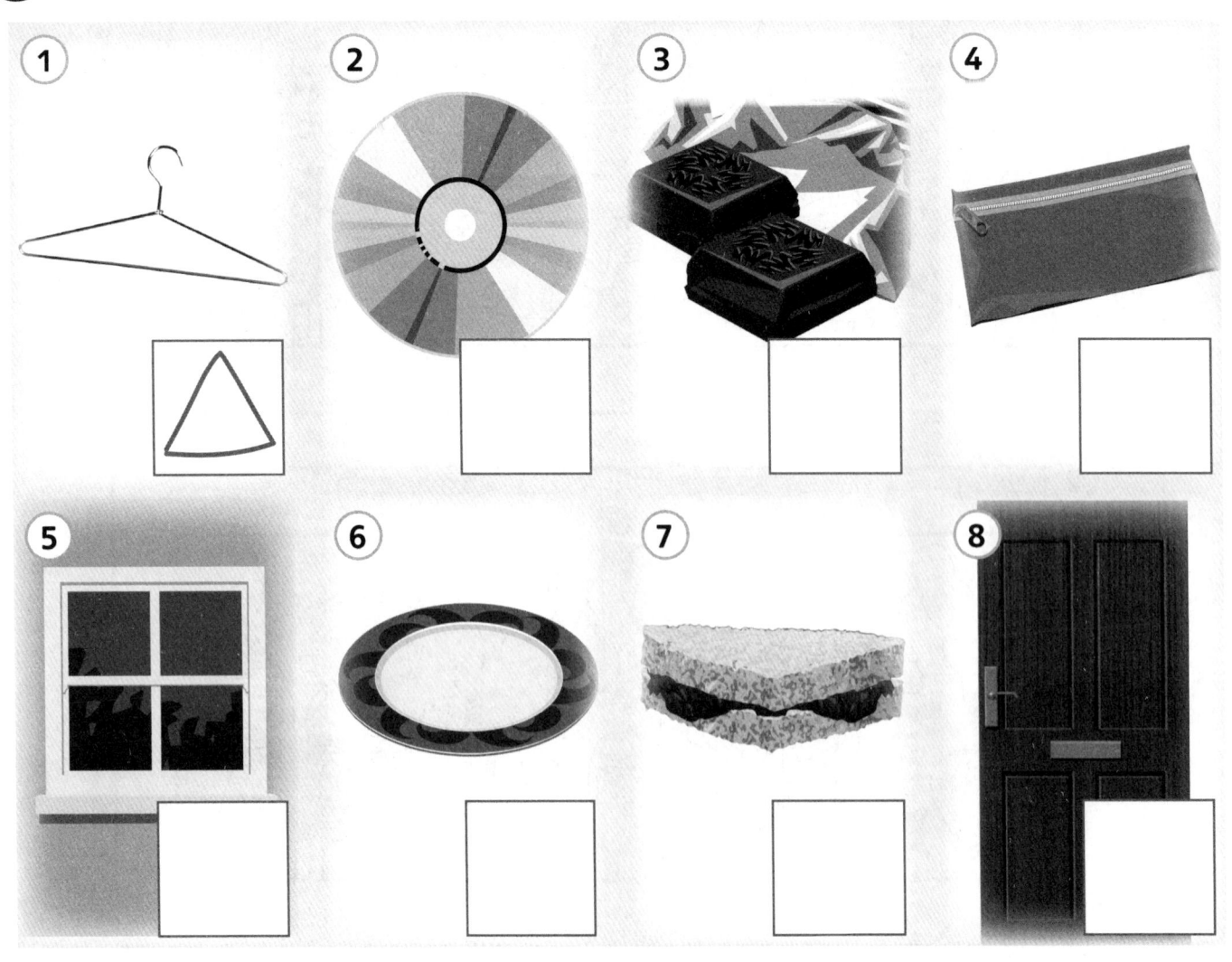

2 Draw and say the shapes. □ △ ▭ ○

84 Math

1 **Think!** Count and circle.

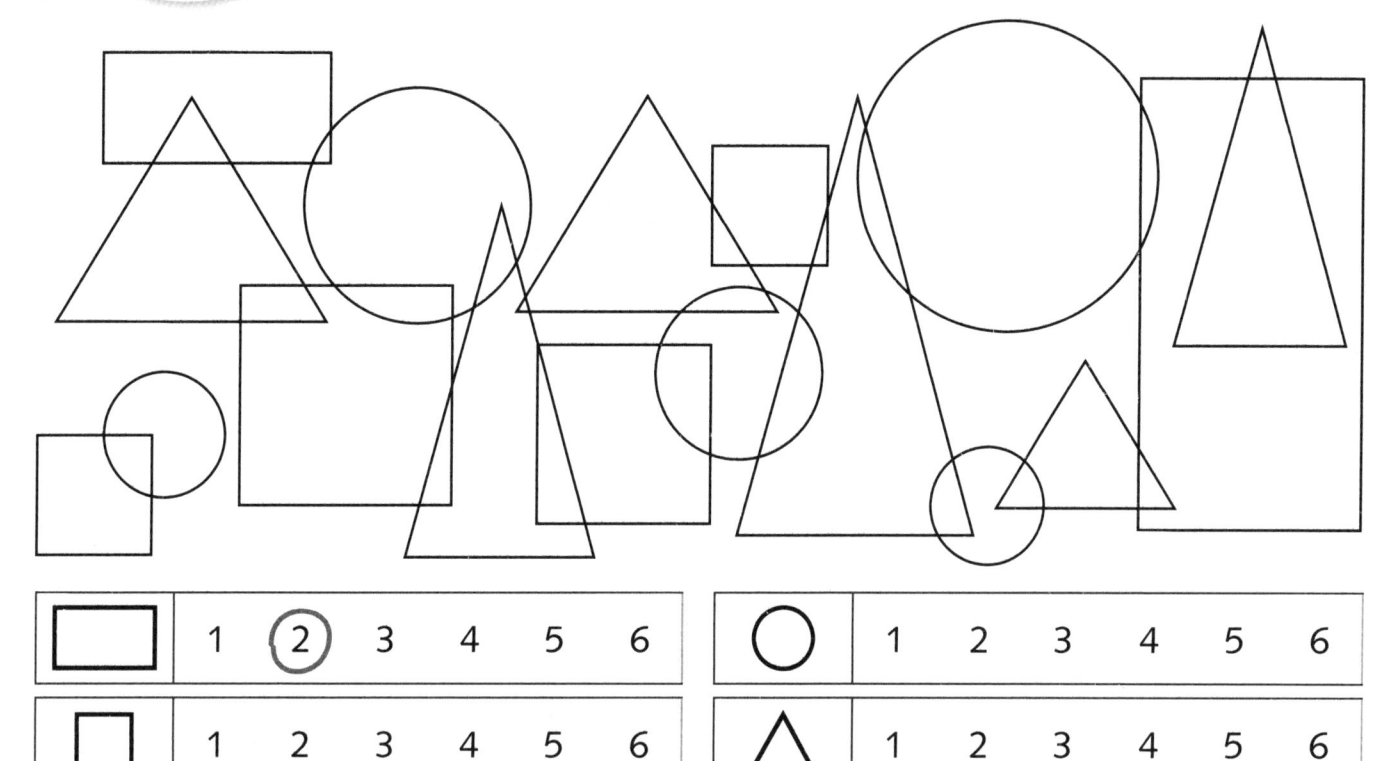

▭	1 (2) 3 4 5 6
□	1 2 3 4 5 6
○	1 2 3 4 5 6
△	1 2 3 4 5 6

2 Listen and color.

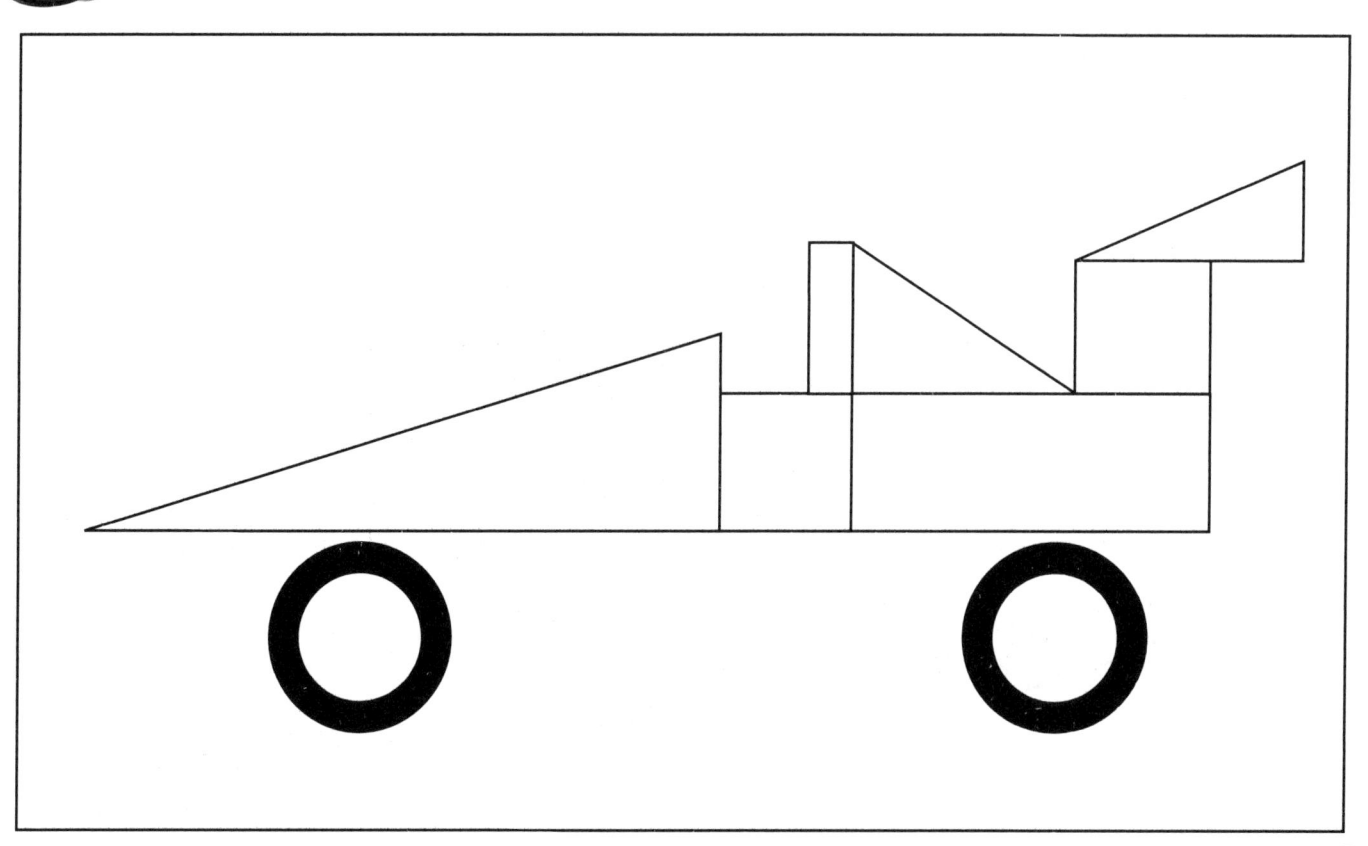

Math 85

1) Have a boat race.

86 Creativity

1 Say the words and trace. Color the circles.

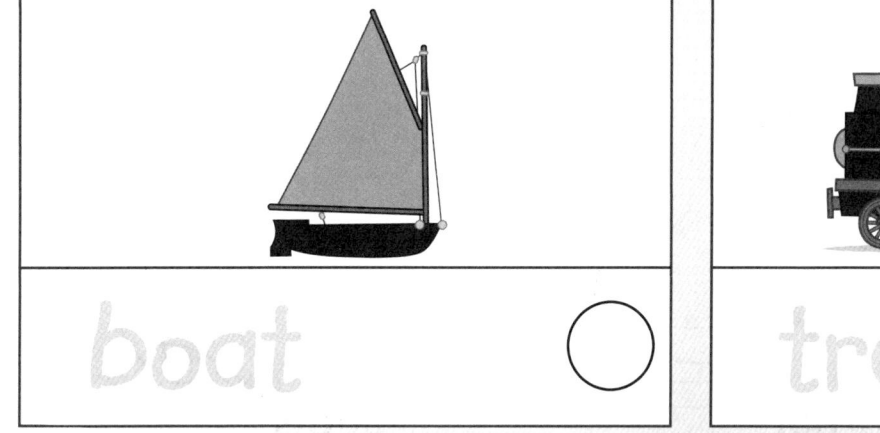

boat

train

car

bike

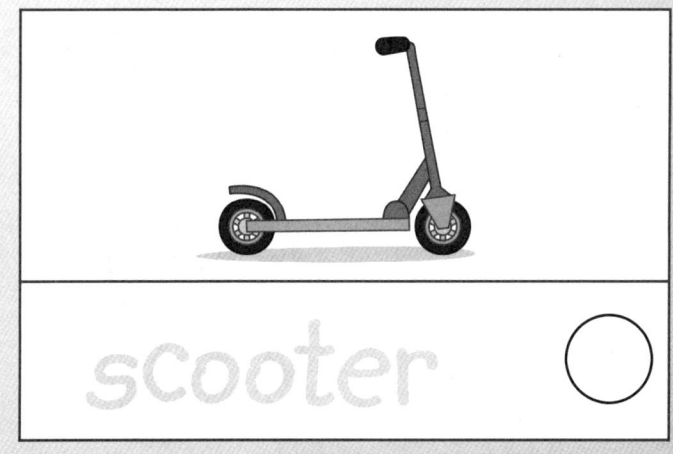

scooter

bus

2 Draw faces. 😊 😐 ☹

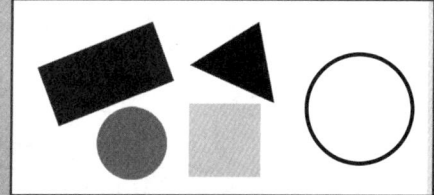

Review 87

9 Party clothes

1 Color and describe.

| shirt | hat | boots |
| shoes | belt | button |

2 Draw five lines. Guess with your friend.

88 hat, belt, boots, shirt, button, shoes

1 **Think!** Follow the food and drink.

I like (cookies, chips, salad, candy).

89

1 Find five differences.

1

2

90 Practice

1 Think! Look and cross out.

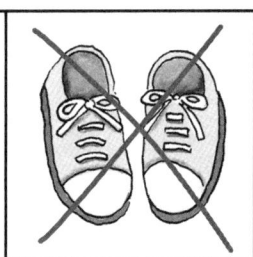

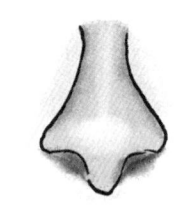

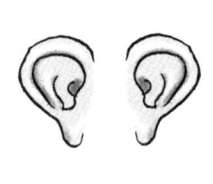

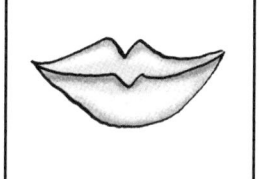

1 Listen and trace.

1

2

3

4

92 Story practice

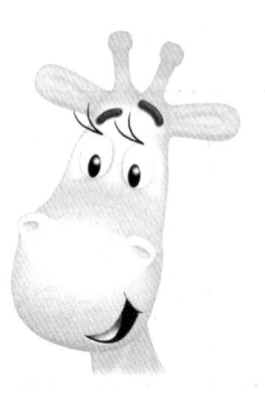

1 Think! Look and color.

1

2

Value: cleaning up 93

1 🎧 Listen and color.

	1	2	3	4	5	6	7	8	9	10

2 Think! Look and color.

1 Color. Follow the lines. Describe the uniforms.

Art 95

1 Make a pirate hat.

96 Creativity

1 Say the words and trace. Color the circles.

shirt

hat

boots

shoes

belt

button

2 Draw faces. 😊 😐 ☹

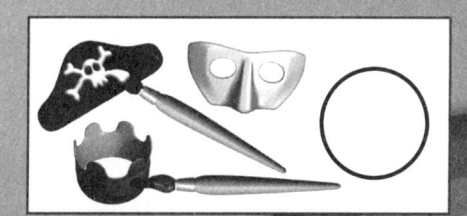

Review 97

Cutouts 99

100 Cutouts

Cutouts 101

102 Cutouts

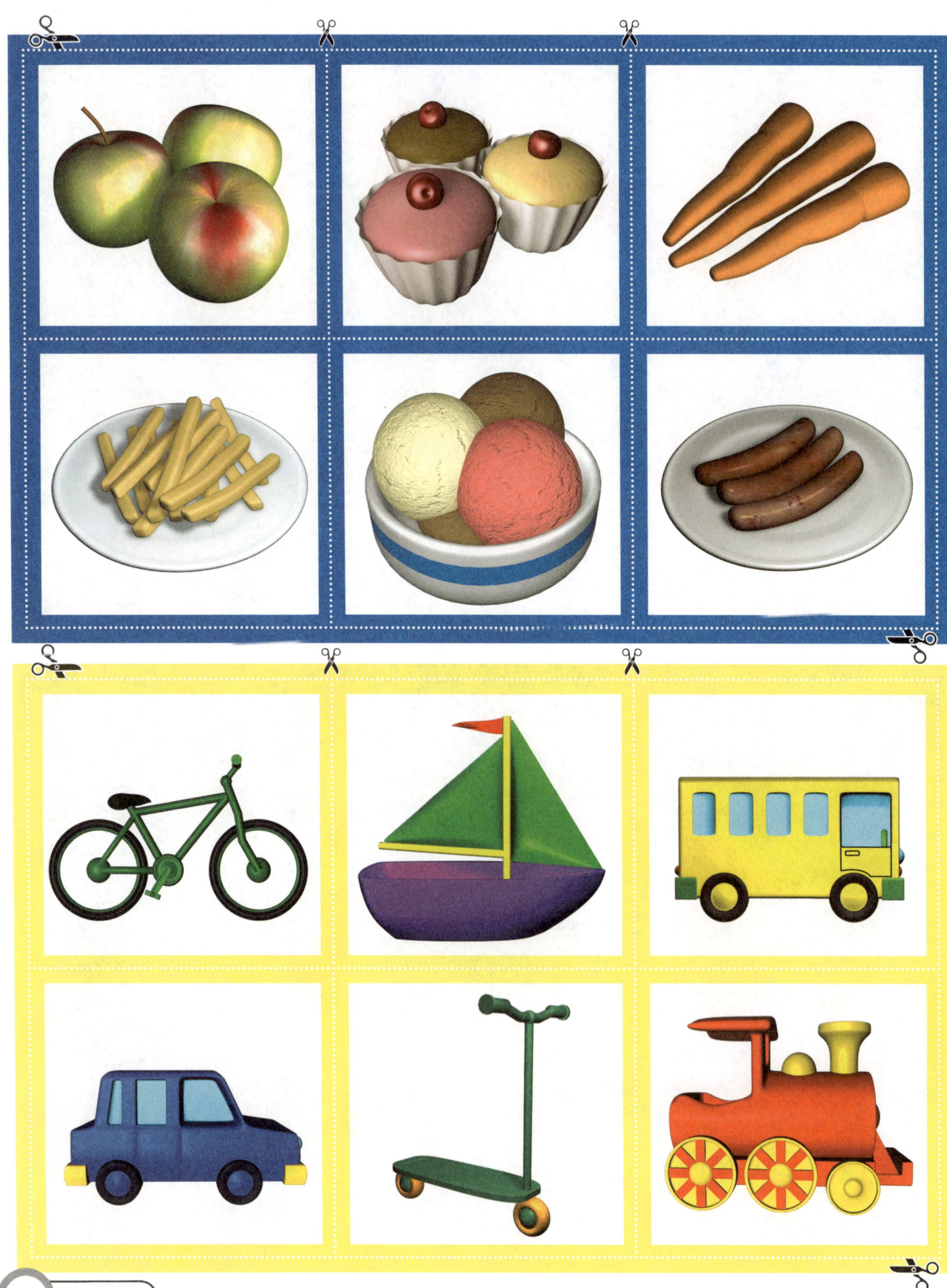

Cutouts

Cutouts

Cutouts 105

106 Cutouts

Cutouts

108 Cutouts

Cutouts

110 Cutouts

Cutouts 111

112 Cutouts